11 SECRETS TO CREATE
TALK-OF-THE-TOWN
LUXURY HOMES

Weaving Love, Life and
INTERIORS AS GLAMOROUS AS YOU

11 SECRETS TO CREATE TALK-OF-THE-TOWN
LUXURY HOMES

Weaving Love, Life and
INTERIORS AS GLAMOROUS AS YOU

SHASHANK JAIN

Worldwide Published by

Pendown Press

PENDOWN PRESS
An ISO 9001 & ISO 14001 Certified Co.,
Regd. Office: 2525/193, 1st Floor, Onkar Nagar-A,
Tri Nagar, Delhi-110035
Ph.: 09350849407, 09312235086
E-mail: info@pendownpress.com
Branch Office: 1A/2A, 20, Hari Sadan, Ansari Road,
Daryaganj, New Delhi-110002
Ph.: 011-45794768
Website: PendownPress.com

First Edition: 2023

ISBN: 978-93-5554-417-9

Layout and Cover Designed by Pendown Graphics Team
Printed and Bound in India by Thomson Press India Ltd.

Content

A Journey
Into The Lap of Luxury

Would you like to create a home that is like none other and that no one has ever seen before? Would you love to design a home that you are proud of inviting guests to? Would you want your home to be as unique as you?

If the answers to the above questions are YES, YES & YES, Hurray, you are holding the right book in your hands!

*"I love transforming spaces into homes
and then into your lifestyle!"*

~Shashank Jain

Hello, my name is Shashank Jain, and I am a "Luxury Home Design Specialist". I was in London many years ago, staying near the London Bridge and travelling the United Kingdom widely.

During my travels, I always wondered about the sophistication of British Design and its proud architectural history, from the grand, neoclassical English Country House and the Georgian Townhouse, to the Farmhouse and the Rustic Cottage style. I explored the entire United Kingdom, from Bournemouth to Inverness in Scotland. I was very much attracted to and influenced by their design and style.

Since childhood, I was very fascinated with popular design books and magazines and thought, what if I could bring these to reality?

Since then, I have wanted to bring that kind of luxury back to Indian homes.

Now I eat, sleep and breathe Interior Design. Combining it with positivity and lifestyle, I am able to express my clients' dreams, desires and lifestyles in their unique homes. Exploring new design ideas on a daily basis continues to top my list of things to do.

Over the years, I have used these hacks and secrets of interior design to successfully complete many high-end projects, and the clients have been delighted beyond measure. They recount that their experiences have been marvelous.

They were so confused at the outset, and then during the home interior design operation, just like a doctor, I was able to bring happiness to their faces and family.

My Journey so far in the design world has been brilliant and rocking!

You must be wondering why I am sharing this book with you. After all, these are practical experiences and secrets which NO Interior Designer would like to share. These hacks and secrets are so powerful and useful that they can empower you to design your home even without hiring an interior designer. Isn't it surprising?

SO, AM I a MONK???

....Naaah...Naa....

The real reason I am sharing this book with you is that:

One, being in love with interior design, I just don't like people being fooled around me easily, So I want to guide and lead most people around me on to the right path of design and a luxurious lifestyle.

Second, Due to time constraints and physical challenges, I can't be present everywhere and help people. My book will help many and indeed bring good KARMA to me (I am happily receiving it) while serving others.

I hope these secrets and hacks will steer you to the path of happiness while designing your next dream home.

So, let's explore the fascinating world of luxury design...

Draw Inspiration From Your Life

How about designing a home that pleases your mind and body? Have you ever thought about it?

Before even thinking of beginning to design your home, write down your lifestyle habits and traits. This is an essential step to creating a rich and expensive home filled with love and compassion. If you go through your life journey from your birth till date. You will find many experiences and events that are responsible for making you the person you are and for everything that you have achieved in life today.

Here are a few areas of life that you can draw inspiration from…

A. **Travel:** We all get inspired by travel, whether in our own country - India or across the world. Travel exposes you to new cultures, people and experiences. Some like to travel solo, some with family and some with friends. Each person or company will bring you a new experience even if you are travelling to the same place repeatedly.

You can think of what all you want to bring to your new home. For example, think about the experience of a London or New York hotel you have always considered bringing to your home. How about a fancy light you really liked while travelling to an amazing cafe in Europe?

Why not bring to your home the sofa pattern you liked while relaxing in a resort? You could also think of adding a plunge pool you really like in the Maldives to give your home a fun vacation feel.

But sometimes, you need help in getting inspired, even from your own life. Here are my effective tips for finding your life inspirations.

To draw inspiration, you can choose an interior design style you liked while you were exploring new places.

Or here is another great way to design. Why not create a specific corner dedicated to the future destination on your list of places you want to visit so that it keeps inspiring you to visit the same while creating a unique design element?

B. **Family and Friends:** These are the people who have inspired you from the beginning. Try talking to them and ask about your childhood and teenage and try to write those experiences on a piece of paper. With this exercise, you will have tons and tons of real-life experiences which can bring you inspiration for your new home.

These are the things of real, non-curated people. The struggles and realness of family that you have been bought up with. All the things which you were dreaming of earlier and are now living with.

There is absolutely no denying the fact that the people you surround yourself with have an undeniable and deep impact on who you become and hence on your home and lifestyle.

When it comes down to the state of mind and people's moods, constant research in the home design space has shown that the devil is in your home interior design and poor planning and colors. Imagine your poor design aesthetics can result in a disturbed, stressful life.

Do you know that light is directly connected to your body's circadian rhythm? Too much or too little light can impact your sleep, mood and, in turn, behavior.

The balancing of energies, as indicated by the Asian practices of Feng Shui,,Vastu etc., impacts the state of mind and body. I am going to cover this as well in this book.

Are you feeling overwhelmed? Have you ever thought about the background work you need to do before even going to your designer? No Designer can do the magic for you if you aren't clear about your life and lifestyle and how you want your home to reflect it.

Whenever I get stuck, I always take a walk and think about the positive change in my life and, where I want to be in life, what I need to learn and create. You can also draw inspiration from the resources shared at the end of the book.

Do remember that your design inspiration should be unique to you. That means what works for one client might not work for you—and vice versa. What matters most is that you find what does work for you and use it to inspire your dream home

Art is Essential

Every piece of art should be carefully selected. Any piece of art can immediately make or break the story of a room or living room. Do you know art pieces in your home add life to a boring space and bring bold elements together.

I am now going to make a very bold statement. Be with me and love me...

In my view, art should be selected first before even designing the color scheme of the room. Selecting the right color mood for your room can be one of the hardest choices you will make in the interior design process.

Once you find a painting or wall hanging that you absolutely love, just don't leave it to the last. Buy it immediately and keep it in your storehouse. You can use that piece as the inspiration for your room's color scheme.

When choosing a piece of wall art to be a focal point for your space, the most important consideration is size.

An artwork that is too small will be lost and overshadowed by the furniture around it, and a piece that is too big will look and stand out as a bad choice. Having the perfect-sized art piece is an act of delicate balance.

Make sure to ask your designer to specify the size of art in the 2D drawings along with wall sizes, so you know how much room you have at your disposal.

For a creative piece to be considered tasteful artwork, it doesn't always have to be super expensive or painted by a famous artist. But yes, artwork from a famous artist does make a bold statement and also enhances luxury.

Any piece of artwork that you can find and that speaks to you is the perfect choice for your space. I always believe art can show your creative side and expose your personality and character.

Do you know there can be many art forms that you can choose from? It can be Wall

Paintings, Frame Art, Sculptures, Digital Art Prints, Murals, and 3D Wall Art, to name a few.

Art is that extra touch that can take your room from simply looking functional and monotone to a well-designed space and speaks for its luxury.

There's always an artwork that represents your style perfectly; you just need to find it. Then, all you need to do is identify an empty wall and proudly showcase your art piece to your friends, family and guests.

Tip: While choosing an art piece, always keep in mind the Interior Design

Style that you've already chosen for the room or your space. Don't be afraid to bring life and creativity into your room.

When it comes to Interior Design, art is always the perfect choice.

Think About
The Flow of Guests

Finding the right materials and products for your luxury home is only half the battle won.

The biggest challenge I foresee is bad layout planning and not thinking about the flow and movement of guests.

Nearly as important as the flow and movement of people around your space is having a consistent, unifying design theme. I have seen many times, even big names in the design world, making one common mistake. They want to place and use all the interior design styles in one house. It not only confuses the guests but depicts your eagerness to show off.

Do you know that just one placement of a sofa can change the entire appearance of the space? One position can lead the guests inside the room and create a welcoming space, while another placement can completely block the room, making you and your guests really uncomfortable.

I know you have money in your pocket and want to buy all the high-end furniture and décor pieces. But hey, hold on for a second and read me out to the full.

When you are shopping for furniture, sofa, consoles, tables, beds, ottomans etc. be sure to leave ample space in between each product. Think of yourself as a guest in your own home and try to visualize the way you will walk in, where you will sit, how you will hold the cup of tea, and where you will keep it. Will it be easy to eat from the plate of cutlets served?

Whenever I work on the design of any home, the first thing I do is relive the space myself first. Think of every action I will do before and after entering this beautifully designed home.

The Key point to note here is it should be easy for you and your guests to freely move around your living space without the need to move around the furniture.

No matter if you are in the bedroom or in your living room, there should always be a focal point in the room. It can be a light fixture, wall art, mural, fireplace, or even a bed — whatever you choose; this should anchor your room. This item should draw attention to the space and work together to bring the entire room together.

What do you want your guest to do and experience in your home? Write down the first few thoughts.

1.

2.

3.

Absolutely, you are the best judge of your friends, family and network habits.

If you want your house to become the talk of the town, just follow your heart and buy the items you like the most. However, don't get carried away by your enthusiasm, Decor items are great, but too many of them can clutter the space.

Ek aur Ram Baan, jab tak cheez showroom mein hai confusion hai, jaise hi wo aapke ghar ke ander ati hai chamak jati hai.

Tip: Designing the right flow of guests encourages intimacy and interaction between you and your guests. It helps you in boosting your home's invitation index. People will be happy coming to your home. They will talk about how welcoming your home feels to others also.

Become French When Using Existing Architecture

Before starting a home construction project, homeowners often wonder whether to hire an architect or an interior designer. The right answer is this-

If you are building from the ground or on a vacant plot or working on an extensive remodel, you will need both.

Even if you are doing luxury interiors for your home, you may need to coordinate with both.

One of the most common mistakes seen is that most Interior designers complain about the existing architecture of the building, villa or flat.

In such situations, the best way to do things is to be inspired by French Architecture. People in France appreciate their centuries-old architecture and use it to enhance the luxury of their interiors and décor.

While most homeowners want to renovate a space to eliminate that sense of wrongness and start afresh, the French use what's off in a home to their benefit, this not only saves extra civil structure cost but also keeps the existing emotions intact if you are renovating.

If you are doing the interiors in a new villa, flat or Farmhouse, then it's a different story. Still, I would suggest not breaking everything and starting from ground zero. You can still use the existing raw walls and structure to create a fresh new look that can be ornamented in luxury.

Though they complement each other, architecture and interior design are separate professions with different training, skillsets, and experiences., So ideally, you might need both professionals to ensure your home construction, remodel, or renovation project goes smoothly. Here are some tips for integrating working with both to run your project smoothly:

Fine Tune your existing architecture if needed.

Facilitate communication between the architect and an interior designer.

Hear both, and don't judge. They both will bring their unique experiences; you need to choose what works best for you.

You can ask for vendors from both architects and interior designers and then choose the best among them and start building or designing your dream home.

Do remember, every home tells a story built by the combined effort and creativity of both the architects and interior designers.

Use Height And Space

If your home isn't blessed with super tall ceilings, you're not alone.

But what if I have good news for you?

Yes, honestly, I do!

We, as Interior designers, have been faking high ceilings for many years, and yes, as I promised, I am sharing these secrets with you.

You can follow these secrets to build the illusion of height and space in your home.

Hang Curtains as high as possible g Instead of hanging the curtains to window height, as usual. You can ask your curtain maker to hang them from the ceiling. If you do so, your eyes will be drawn to the height, and you will perceive the room as higher.

Use Low Height Furniture

This is one of my biggest secrets whenever I don't see an opportunity to make a room look taller. I go for low-height furniture, starting with your sofa, beds, center table and so on.

Use stripe patterns on your wall and furniture

The key to making your room height taller is to keep your eyes upwards. There are many patterns, but the most efficient one is to use stripes anywhere and everywhere.

Hang Mirrors higher than usual **g** Mirrors are great friends when discussing interiors. We play a lot with them. When there is cramped space, use the reflective property of mirrors to make your room look spacious and taller.

Use fewer False Ceilings and more natural tones

I know you want to disagree with me here. But this is a fact, the more height you will use in the false ceilings, the lesser will be the space available for you to use in the room. Even if you have a big room, it will still feel very small. I recommend flush-mounted structures, lighting or ceilings to create a feeling of space and height.

Use light-toned furniture

To prevent your room from appearing ultra-busy, stick with neutral or light shades of furniture. But don't worry: That doesn't mean you have to go completely white or light. I know this is not possible in India. But I personallylove a lot of whites and grays. You can add a pop of colors through your accents, like your pillows, rugs, paintings, accessories and decor.

Declutter or free up the space

This is one of my favorite action items. Most of the ladies hate me for this. I always say reduce the furniture and storage and declutter the space. As you all know, We Indians are masters of storage. We can find storage anywhere and everywhere. But believe it or not, you can declutter the room and feel the immediate effect. A clean, organized room makes your whole space feel bright, airy, and spacious.

Accessorizing With Metal

Luxury home design is traditionally associated with luxe metals like gold, silver, bronze and copper. Metallic accents have a huge effect on home luxury, especially when mixed with other materials such as wood, glass, marble and fabrics like velvet, silk etc. It instantly makes a home look glamorous.

But be careful not to go overboard, as it can spoil the overall look and make it look tacky or gaudy.

Use them sparingly, and wait to see the magic they create in your home. Here are my tips for accessorizing your home with the best possible materials available today.

Adding Gold or Rose Gold elements to your home

I always say this to my clients, add some drama and contrast to your home. Metal elements help achieve this in a bold way. How much you want to add depends upon the taste you have.

Different patterns, profiles, elements, textures and shades can be added that induce the look with class and a sense of luxury.

Feature Wall

A feature wall for your living room will help you stand out from your neighbor. It quickly adds luxury to modern living. It may not cover your entire wall, yet an element of style should be there. A wall-to-wall bookshelf, a floor-to-ceiling dresser, a full-height crockery cabinet – all of these grand furniture pieces can enhance the feature status. Let this be the area where most of your décor pieces go, and this wall will surely add character to your room.

Marble combined with metal accents

We have been traditionally hearing about marble. Today, there is so much variety available that you can't even imagine.

The patterns are really something to look upon. When Italian marble is combined with Gold Brass aesthetics in a strong feature living room wall, the results are just WOW!. The Brass can be finished in many different metal finishes, creating a truly unique and jaw-dropping experience for your visitors.

Be creative in mixing metals

I love playing with different metals, finishes and tones. Sometimes, my vendors complain about the hard work required in putting this to execution. Mixing texture creates a personalized and unique space that no one has seen. I also like to add some polishes and matte finishes together. They can create such a wonderful experience for the user. Adding a brass object, floor lamp, or table bowl is a great way to add luxury without worrying about it overpowering a room.

Hence, whenever you see a bold metal element or an object, don't run away; just grab it.

Not Spending It All

It takes time and life experience to design and decorate a home. After all, it is the one place you look forward to coming back to every night.

Just because it looks good, it need not cost a fortune. I always have a habit of saying what is right and what is not, so I don't shy away from saying that I believe even after spending tons of money, your home may not look good.

Do you know why?

Because it lacks energy, and you and your designer didn't try to steal a deal. Money does not always bring happiness. Neither does it automatically result in great design aesthetics. When buying, you need to choose what you like, what will look good, and what will it be beneficial to buy at this price.

Hey.. Don't get me wrong. I am not saying that you shouldn't spend at all. My simple take is to be wise and spend where it is absolutely necessary, and use it where it can be managed.

Being resourceful when looking to take advantage of trusted interior design secrets will pay you off or when bringing the best furnishings into your home without having to spend a ton is the key.

Interior design is no longer just a luxury for the ultra-rich of our country, such as the Adanis, Ambanis or Singhanias. Back in 2000, only 1% of the population could afford an interior designer.

Now, Interior designing is becoming a solid investment for many. No matter whether you're an individual homeowner seeking to renovate your home or a realtor looking to increase the value of your property portfolio, investing in luxury interior design can be a great way to stand out from the crowd.

Let me share with you some more secrets of how wise spending can be beneficial to you.

1. **Adds value to your property**: By investing in some luxury interior finishes, you will be improving the value of your property and making a great return on your investment both from an emotional value and financial standpoint.

2. **Adds comfort and elegance**: The Interiors of your home can make your living easy and comfortable. You should invest in a good sofa and bed that can adjust with some finishes in a wardrobe, as a sofa and bed impact your comfort and wellbeing more than a wardrobe.

3. **Talk of the Town:** If you have a habit of investing in luxurious interiors of your home and seek some little changes over the course of time, your home will always be the talk of the town. I am not asking you to renovate every year, but you can simply add some decor, soft furnishings, bedsheets, update wallpaper etc. in a couple of years.

4. **Pat on your back:** Owning a house is not that easy today. The skyrocketing real estate prices and our lifestyles sometimes do not allow us to buy what we desire.

Congratulations on owning such a great property. Just keep in mind, while doing your interiors, you may add 5 pieces to your house, but those should be high on quality and class. You may spend on the next 5 pieces next year.

Hence, don't become "penny wise and pound foolish". Where-ever it is needed to spend, spend it all but keep in mind you have to balance the home with the right amount of luxury without getting into debt or borrowing money from your friends and family.

Use Luxury Mirrors

Luxury Mirrors are very important and remarkable pieces in enhancing the luxury of the bedroom or living room. For any room decoration, you just need the magic of Luxury Mirrors.

The large round wall lamp sculpture in the picture above is a great example of creating luxury through mirrors. It is made of wood folded by polished stainless steel,which portrays a perfect mirror. Are you surprised? I am sure you are!

This majestic wall mirror lamp is a soulful piece with classic distinction for outstanding luxury homes.

Truly the embodiment of a fairytale, this Luxury Mirror is what dreams are made of.

Perfect for a neo-classical bedroom or a foyer, this furniture element will make you feel like royalty.

The Lapiaz Round Mirror takes exceptional craftsmanship and design to a new realm. Bringing beauty in the most unexpected places, this contemporary design piece is inspired by authentic karst formations created by surface dissolution, freezing, or thawing of limestone or dolomite rocks. Is it too confusing?

Don't worry; I am confused too...What matters is the gorgeous end result. Just take a look at this magical mirror and see how you can get this in your home.

Last but not least, you can use simple mirrors fused with some gold and bronze accents to enhance the space. There are two components to be noted here. One is the The bed back mirror and the other one is the console mirror. Both are symmetric in design and help you add luxury to the entire space.

Create Statement Elements with Lighting

Gone are those days when you would want to take a crystal chandelier for your lighting. Nowadays, one of the key ways to make a statement in your interiors is through lighting design. The world's best designers are increasingly using light fixtures as the central artistic piece of the room. I have also been doing it for many years.

A lot of designs find inspiration from nature, be it clouds or branches. Numerous styles are purely geometric and abstract, and I love all of them.

What do you think about the chandelier in the picture? Can you take a guess as to how it would have been crafted? Gold bars infused with lights give you a perfect statement lighting piece. This can be used at various places in the house. Whether it is a double-height drawing room or a dining space, this is a piece everyone would desire.

This amazing piece in the picture above is called the Newton Suspension Lamp, a handcrafted piece which has a story to tell in every house. I called this a monumental piece which depicts the luxury and capacity of delightful, skilled artisans. I was so in love with this that I tried exploring it in India and called my vendors to make one for me.

There are many such elements and designs that can help you enhance the luxury and will surely make a bold statement for your guests. I can write for even the next 20 pages about all of my secret art and light collection.

However, if I share everything with you here, then perhaps I would miss the opportunity of meeting you personally. So, I am keeping those for when we meet to bring your luxurious dream home to life together.

Colors That Control
Your Subconscious

Believe it or not, the choices that you make when deciding how your home will look have a deep effect on your emotions while living in the house.

I am sure that you could never have imagined that the color of your kitchen might be contributing to your anxiety. Before now, I am sure you would never have thought about it. Close your eyes for a minute and think about the kitchen you are living in.

Are you happy? Are you anxious? Are you confused? If the answer to any of the above questions is yes. That's good because you are now going to hack your subconscious brain.

As you begin thinking about your luxury home interior design, make sure that you are using colors that can help you tone the space to make it healing, relaxing and calming.

Modern color psychology dates its origins to the early 19thcentury when JohannWolfgang von Goethe published his book, Theory of Colours. If you want to learn more about colors this is the book you can buy on amazon.

Now, let me take you on a journey to the psychological side of décor.

- White relates to a sense of cleanliness and purity. It is great for defining a space, but use white in combination with other colors since too much white is neither practical nor acceptable here in India.

- Black symbolizes power. Use black for statement pieces that you want to draw the eye to.

- Brown or Beige is connected to natural roots, just like a tree, and it provides a relaxing touch. It connects us to the ground and doesn't allow us to be overly affected by show-sha. It also helps us keep our tones earthy. You can choose it for rooms where the family groups and for places like the parent's bedroom.

- Gray color is one of my favorites, and it gives a sense of relaxation and serenity. Use gray in spaces like home offices or bathrooms. You may also think of putting it in your master bedroom.

- Blue enhances the feelings of calm and freshness. It's a good fit for high-flow areas like kitchens and bathrooms.

- Green is always known for its soothing qualities. Green is the perfect choice for a foyer or entryway because it eases the transition from the outside. Whenever you think of green, what do you feel? Peace & calm, right? It makes you feel like all is well with the world.

Yellow is a color that is associated with happiness, creation, and creativity. It works well in combination with neutral colors and in rooms with lots of natural light to create a peaceful environment for your space.

Orange offers a boost of energy and innovation. It's best used as an accent because too much can leave people feeling overwhelmed. I just love the accents of Orange.

Red symbolizes love, power and passion. It can be used to warm up spaces and make them feel more intimate. You can use them in your master bedroom or maybe in the lounge.

Lilac (a lighter Shade of purple) has recently taken the limelight. This color connects with royalty and luxury. It is a great choice for formal living rooms or master bedrooms because it adds an element of class and sophistication.

Do remember, when you choose which colors to be included in your interior space, three picks are better than one.

Hey, wait ☺ I am not saying to add all three to the same room. You can make a little combination of all three. For example, choose a neutral for the bigger items like walls and flooring, a calmer color for furniture and then pick a third more dramatic color to pop in your statement accessories and décor. I always suggest you pick colors based on what mood you have selected for the desired space.

Use Timeless Furniture

Inspiration is the key to starting a new luxury interior design project. So here I am sharing with you some amazing inspiration. Contrasting in style but converging with unique furniture, these elegant modern pieces are breathtaking and ready to inspire you. Enjoy!

I am loving presenting these to you here.

Use this dark bedroomas a starting point for your next luxury home. Ideal for a luxury bedroom, this brilliantly designed side table and a gold resin-infused bed are a kill in itself.

If I were your guest, I am sure I would want to borrow or steal for my bedroom.

All-white interiors are like a blank canvas, and I love it. It really gives you a chance to express your personality. This wood nightstand reallypops in the middle of this soothing master bedroom.

You must be wondering how can a mere side table enhance luxury. Shashank, are you kidding me?

The answer to this cannot be summed up in just one word. There are many factors to it, not just one.

If you have read my complete book, you will be able to understand the deep technicality behind it.

Here, I am showing you a glimpse of a bathroom. This is one vanity with a classic mirror. A contemporary bathroom with big wall mirrors. The golden color of the furniture lightens the room and creates a nice contrast with the dark marbled floor.

As you can see, if you try to think of luxury, every element of the house plays a vital role. I don't want to overwhelm you here, but there are many more pieces to this puzzle.

Meet me personally, and I will be happy to help you put together the pieces of this design puzzle to get the most amazing results.

I am sure not a lot of pieces can be paired with this blue diamond console. It's an art in itself, skillfully designed and executed to perfection. What are your thoughts about this?

Hence, whenever you want to go upscale the luxury of your home, timeless furniture is one of the most important elements you should not overlook.

I always say this to my clients, Invest wherever it is absolutely necessary and go affordable wherever you can. This is how you can have a perfect budget for everything you desire in the home.

I could not stop myself from sharing this masterpiece. The colors, art, furniture, lighting, and rug give me a sense of satisfaction and luxury.

If you have this as your casual seat, why would you ever go to a Dubai Hotel and explore the luxury outside?

So,think and plan carefully about the furniture you will buy in your next dream home, whether it will just be placed in any corner of the room or will it enhance, beautify or add a sense of luxury to your space.

Luxury is not only what you desire; it is also what you deserve!

You deserve a space that is as much the talk of the town as it is the solace of your heart. A space that keeps you calm, relaxed and motivated and also welcomes guests with warmth and style, making them feel at home while amazing them with its uniqueness.

Go ahead and use the professional secrets and tips I have shared with you to transform your space with amazing results.

And for those of you who want to settle for nothing less than the "Best of the Best", set up a discovery call with my team and me at the link and numbers given below. Despite our packed schedules, we promise to revert within 48 hours.

Yours sincerely in luxury

~Shashank Jain